CONTENTS

WHAT WAS A PTEROSAUR?

An animal soars high over the heads of dinosaurs. Its long wings flap once. It **glides** out over the ocean. Suddenly, it swoops down! The animal's long beak reaches into the water. It comes up holding a flapping fish. Is this hunter a bird? A dinosaur? Nope. It's a pterosaur!

21st Century Junior Library

DISCOVER THE PTEROSAUR

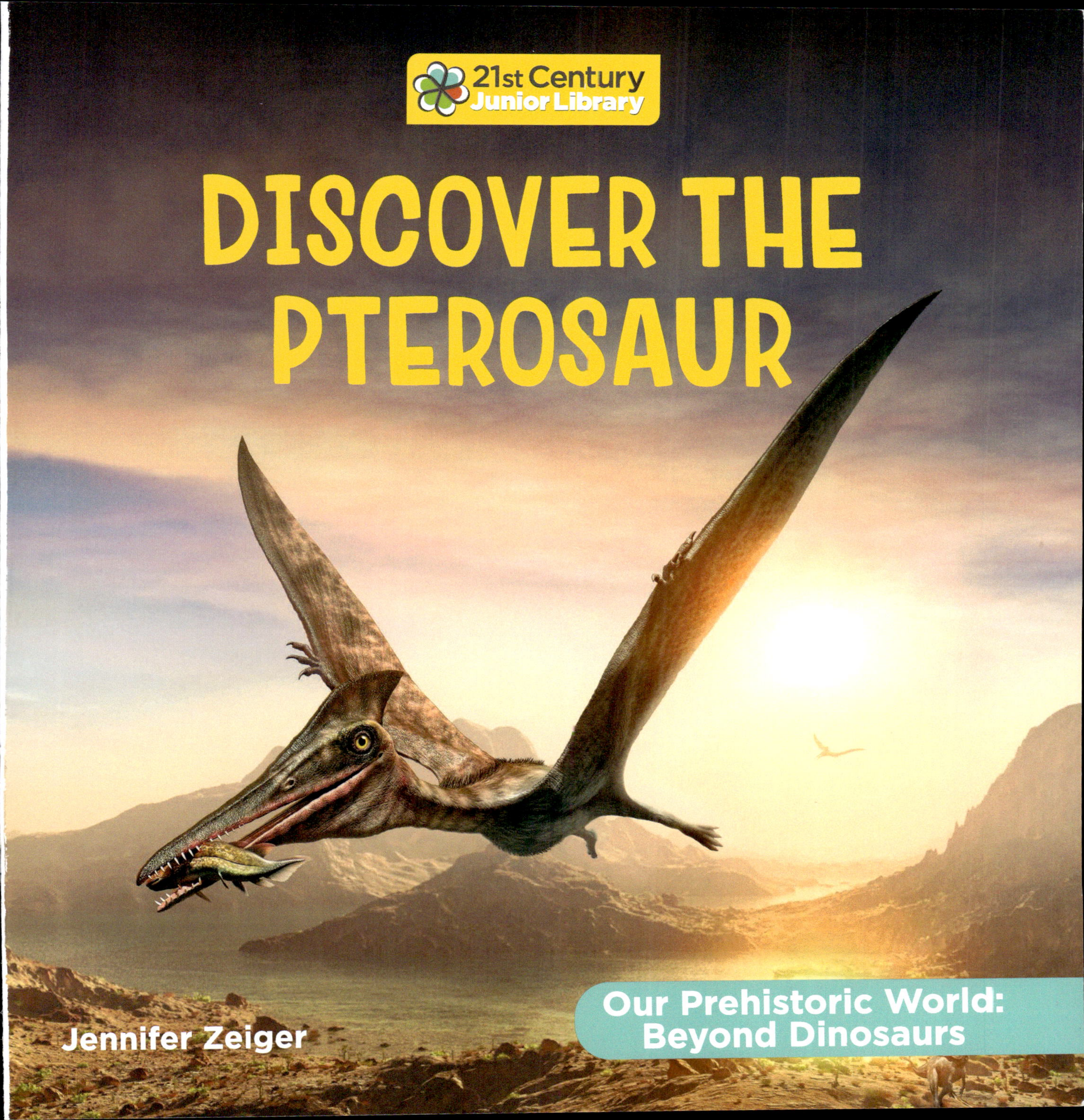

Jennifer Zeiger

Our Prehistoric World: Beyond Dinosaurs

Published in the United States of America by:

Cherry Lake Press
2395 South Huron Parkway, Suite 200, Ann Arbor, Michigan 48104
www.cherrylakepress.com

Content Adviser: Gregory M. Erickson, PhD, Dinosaur Paleontologist, Department of Biological Science, Florida State University, Tallahassee, Florida

Reading Adviser: Beth Walker Gambro, MS, Ed., Reading Consultant, Yorkville, IL

Photo and Illustration Credits: © Warpaint/Shutterstock, cover, title page; © Illustration by Brian Engh, 5; © Mark Witton, 6; © Illustration by Brian Engh, 7; © Illustration by Brian Engh, 8–9; © satori13/iStock.com, 10; © Imago by Zhao Chuang/Alamy, 11; © CoreyFord/iStock.com, 12; © YuRi Photolife/Shutterstock,13; © Mark Witton, 14; © Warpaintcobra/iStock.com, 16–17; © Warpaintcobra/iStock.com, 18–19; © YuRi Photolife/Shutterstock, 20–21

Cherry Lake Press is an imprint of Cherry Lake Publishing Group.

Library of Congress Cataloging-in-Publication Data has been filed and is available at catalog.loc.gov.

Cherry Lake Press would like to acknowledge the work of the Partnership for 21st Century Learning, a Network of Battelle for Kids. Please visit Battelle for Kids online for more information.

Printed in the United States of America

Cherry Lake Press

Fish were a favorite meal for pterosaurs!

Pterosaurs were flying **reptiles**. They were not dinosaurs. But they were around at the same time as dinosaurs. Pterosaurs lived between 228 million and 66 million years ago. They were found around the world. You will not see any living

***Caviramus* was a pterosaur with a powerful bite.**

pterosaurs now, though. They are **extinct**.

Birds are dinosaurs' living **descendants**.

The pterosaur doesn't have any.

Make a Guess!

Dinosaurs and pterosaurs were both reptiles. Do you think flying is the only thing that makes them different? With an adult, go online and find out if you're right!

WHAT DID A PTEROSAUR LOOK LIKE?

Most pterosaurs had short bodies. They had long necks and beaks. Many had head **crests**. Some pterosaurs had tails. Others had no tail at all. Their back legs were long and thin like a bird's. Their feet had sharp, curved claws. Pterosaurs likely had feathers. They may even have had brightly colored feathers.

Caviramus had a crest. Some scientists think crests helped pterosaurs identify members of their own species.

One part of each wing connected to a pterosaur's body. The other part stretched along the arm to the tip of a very long finger. When a pterosaur stuck its arms out, its wings stretched out.

Look!

Look at a picture of a pterosaur. Then look up pictures of reptiles alive today. What does a pterosaur have in common with them? How is it different?

Different kinds of pterosaurs were different sizes. Some were as small as sparrows. Others were much bigger. The largest had wings that stretched more than 36 feet (11 meters) across. It was the largest flying animal ever.

Small pterosaurs could likely fly soon after birth. But larger pterosaurs had to live on the ground and grow before learning to fly.

Tupdandactylus was a type of pterosaur that also spent a good deal of time on the ground.

HOW DID A PTEROSAUR LIVE?

Pterosaurs were **predators**. They ate meat. Pterosaurs had very good eyesight. They could spot **prey** while flying high above.

Some pterosaurs lived near the water. They probably ate fish and other water animals.

There were also pterosaurs that ate bugs and other small land animals. The largest pterosaurs may have eaten dead animals, including dinosaurs.

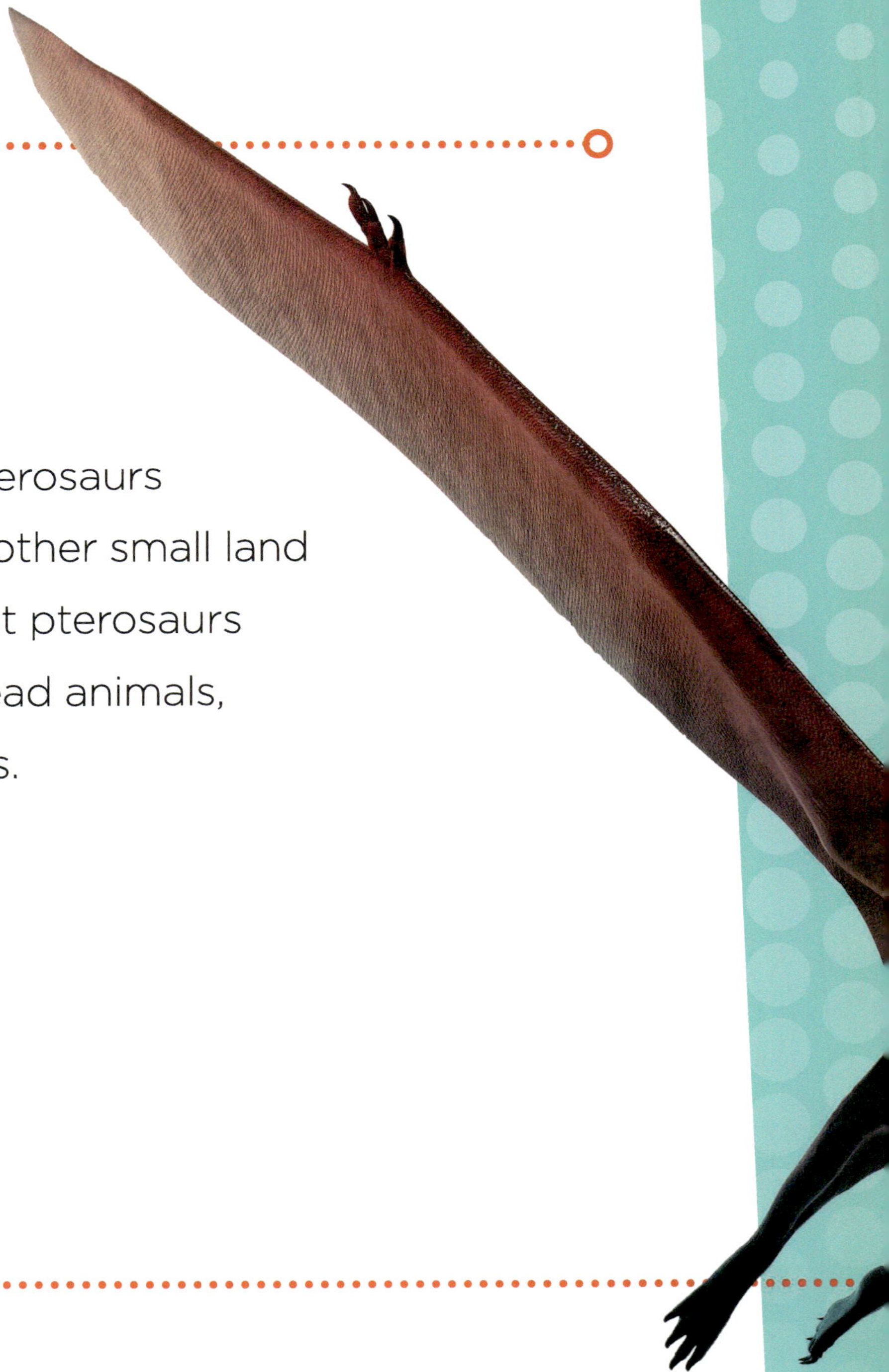

Scientists can tell what pterosaurs ate from fossils. They study fossilized stomach contents. They study pterosaur beaks and teeth.

Anhanguera was another fish-eating pterosaur. It lived between 112 million and 93 million years ago.

Some pterosaurs had short, sharp teeth. They could grip slippery fish or other prey. Other pterosaurs had long, thin teeth. These predators could grab mouthfuls of water with sea animals in it. The water flowed out between the pterosaur's teeth. The sea animals stayed inside the predator's mouth. Some pterosaurs had no teeth. Experts think they swallowed fish whole.

We know about pterosaurs from **fossils**. The first pterosaur fossil was found in 1784. Since then, many more have been found. Some fossils are bones.

Scientists also think that pterosaur crests may have been used to attract mates.

Others are footprints or other remains. Each new fossil holds clues to how these animals lived. There is always more to learn. Someday you could make pterosaur discoveries!

Ask Questions!

What else do you want to know about pterosaurs? Write your questions down. Read more to find answers. Ask a trusted adult to help find answers in scientific articles.

GLOSSARY

crests (KRESTS) bumps on animals' skulls formed by bone or tufts of feathers, fur, or skin

descendants (dih-SEN-duhnts) children or offspring of someone or something from long ago

extinct (ik-STINKT) no longer found living anywhere on Earth

fossils (FAH-suhlz) remains or traces of plants, animals, and other living things that have been preserved as rocks

glides (GLIDEZ) soars on wind currents without flapping

predators (PREH-duh-tuhrz) animals that hunt other animals for food

prey (PRAY) animals that are hunted by other animals for food

reptiles (REP-tielz) cold-blooded animals that have backbones and reproduce by laying eggs

FIND OUT MORE

Books

Austen, Lily. *Pterosaur*. Minneapolis, MN: Jump!, 2025.

Pallotta, Jerry. *Who Would Win?: Ultimate Pterosaur Rumble.* New York, NY: Scholastic, 2025.

Websites

With an adult, learn more online with these suggested searches.

Kiddle: Pterosaur facts for kids

Explore different kinds of pterosaurs and how they flew.

Science Journal for Kids: Where did flying reptiles come from?

Explore facts and watch videos to find out more about pterosaurs.

INDEX

ABOUT THE AUTHOR

Jennifer Zeiger lives in Chicago, Illinois. She writes and edits children's books on all sorts of topics.

ABOUT PALEOARTISTS

Paleoartists bring the prehistoric world to life! They work with scientists, paleontologists, museums, and their own research to recreate living things from long, long ago. **Mark Witton** is one paleoartist featured in this series. He has been studying prehistoric creatures for over 20 years! **Brian Engh** is another. He builds sculptures, too. He designs and builds whole exhibits. He started Living Relic Productions.